The life cycle of

Rose

Ruth Thomson

WAYLAND

First published in paperback in 2013 by Wayland

Copyright © Wayland 2013

Wayland
338 Euston Road
London NW1 3BH

Wayland Australia
Level 17/207 Kent Street
Sydney, NSW 2000

Editor: Clare Lewis
Designer: Simon Morse
Consultant: Michael Scott OBE, B.Sc

Photographs: Cover (inset mr and br), 3, 7, 8, 12, 14, 18,
20, 21, 23tl, 23 br, 23bl naturepl.com; Cover (main) Mark
Hicken/Alamy; Cover (inset tr), 10 Brian Hoffman/Alamy;
2 Imagebroker/Alamy; 4-5 Stone Nature
Photography/Alamy; 6 Frank Blackburn/Alamy;
9 Michael Wheatley/Alamy; 11, 23tr Marilyn
Shenton/Alamy;13 Leonid Serebrennikov/Alamy;
15 Premaphotos/Alamy; 16 Organica/Alamy;
17 Neil Thomson; 19 WoodyStock/Alamy;
22 blickwinkel/Alamy.

British Library Cataloguing in Publication Data
Thomson, Ruth
    The life cycle of a rose. - (Learning about life cycles)
    1. Roses - Life cycles - Juvenile literature
    I. Title
    583.7'34
ISBN: 978-0-7502-7186-8

Printed and bound in China

Wayland is a division of Hachette Children's Books, an
Hachette UK company
www.hachette.co.uk

Contents

Roses grow here

People plant roses in gardens and parks. Wild roses grow on hedges in the countryside.

What is a rose?

A rose is a flowering plant. They usually have stems with sharp thorns. Garden roses have large, colourful flowers. Many have a strong, sweet smell.

A garden rose ▶

leaf

petal

thorn

stem

A wild rose ▲

thorn

Wild roses have
smaller flowers.
This books looks
at wild roses.

7

Seeds and shoots

Rose plants grow from **seeds**. In spring, warm weather and rain help the seed to sprout. Slowly, a shoot pushes up through the ground.

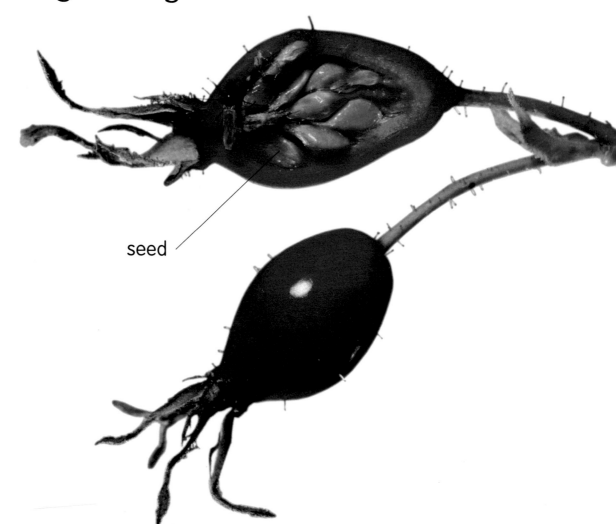

seed

The new plant grows bigger
and bigger. It climbs up a hedge
or tree to reach the light.
Its **thorns** help it to hang on.

May

Buds

New leaves appear. New flower **buds** begin to grow.

Green **sepals** protect the flower buds.
Soon the sepals open out, showing
the petals inside.

Sepal

Flowers

Each flower has five petals with a sweet scent. It also has a sweet liquid called **nectar**.

June-August

petal

pollen

The flowers produce tiny grains
called **pollen**. This is needed
to make **seeds**.

Pollination

A flower's scent attracts insects, such as beetles, flies and bees. As they feed on the **nectar**, **pollen** sticks to them.

When an insect goes to another flower, pollen from the first flower rubs off onto the next one. This is called pollination.

Receptacle

After pollination, the flower no longer needs to attract insects. Its petals fall off.

The top part of the stem,
called the receptacle,
starts to swell. **Seeds**
begin to grow inside it.

receptacle

Rosehip

The receptacle swells more and turns red. Once it is ripe, it is called a rosehip.

The rosehip is packed with **seeds**.
These have a very tough coat
to protect them.

seed

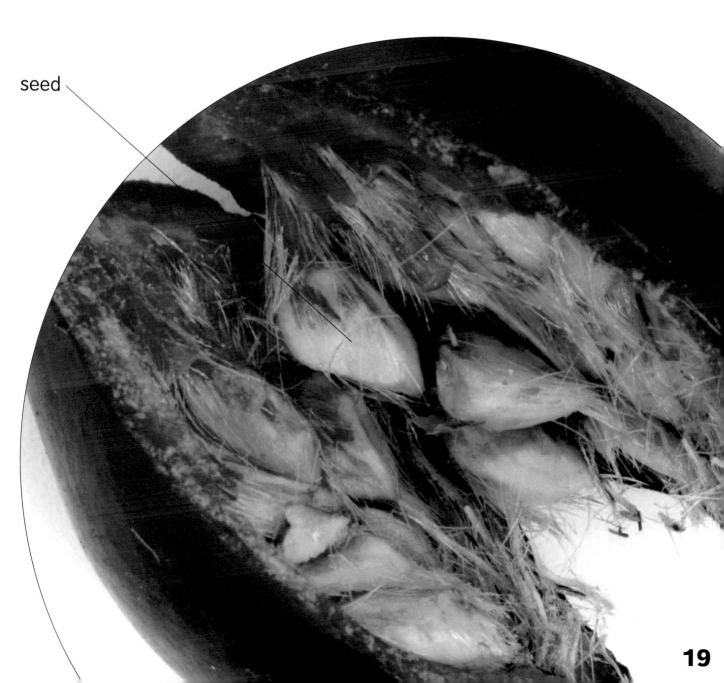

Seeds

Bright, glossy rosehips are a good food for small animals and birds. They often carry the rosehips away from the plant.

The **seeds** come out unharmed
in bird and animal droppings.
They may land on soil where they
can grow into new rose plants.

Autumn and winter

The rosehips stay on the plant at the beginning of winter. They make a tasty meal for hungry birds and are soon eaten up. In the spring, new leaves begin growing again.

Rose life cycle

Seed
In the spring, a tiny
seed starts to grow
into a new plant.

Buds
Leaf and flower
buds appear
on the plant.

Rosehip
After a flower is pollinated,
a rosehip starts to form.
Seeds are growing inside.

Flowers
The flower
buds open.

Glossary

bud the part of a plant from which leaves or flowers develop

nectar the sweet liquid inside many flowers that attracts insects

pollen the grains of powder in flowers needed to make new seeds

seed the part of a plant that grows into a new plant

sepal the part of a plant that wraps around a bud to keep it safe before it opens

thorn hard pointed part of a plant that grows on the stem

Index